Systems of
Government

DEMOCRACY

Sean Connolly

A+

Smart Apple Media

Published by Smart Apple Media, an imprint of Black Rabbit Books
P. O. Box 3263, Mankato, Minnesota 56002
www.blackrabbitbooks.com

Library of Congress Cataloging-in-Publication Data
Connolly, Sean, 1956-
 Democracy / Sean Connolly.
       p. cm. — (Systems of government)
 Includes index.
 Summary: "Describes the workings of a democratic government, including the differences
between a constitutional monarchy, a parliamentary democracy, and a presidential
democracy. Includes discussions on the benefits of direct and indirect democracies, points
out weak points of democracy, and looks to the future of how other countries will continue
to strive to be democratic"—Provided by publisher.
 ISBN 978-1-59920-803-9 (library binding)
 1. Democracy—Juvenile literature. I. Title.
 JC423.C692 2013
 321.8—dc23
                              2011040096

Created by Appleseed Editions, Ltd.
Designed by Hel James
Edited by Mary-Jane Wilkins
Picture research by Su Alexander

Picture credits
page 5 India Today Group/Getty Images; 7 AFP/Getty Images; 9 Farrell Grehan/Corbis;
10 Popperfoto/Getty Images; 12 India Today Group/Getty Images; 14 Getty Images;
17 AFP/Getty Images; 18 Shutterstock; 20 Getty Images; 21 & 23 AFP/Getty Images;
24, 26, 28, 29, 30, 32 & 34 Getty Images; 36 CBS via Getty Images; 38 & 39 AFP/Getty
Images; 40 Shutterstock; 42 Globo via Getty Images; 44 AFP/Getty Images

Printed in the United States of America at Corporate Graphics, North Mankato, Minnesota

PO1445
2-2012

9 8 7 6 5 4 3 2 1

Contents

What Is Democracy?

The statesman Winston Churchill had an unexpected and often humorous way of expressing basic truths. Speaking in the British House of Commons in November 1947, he declared: "Democracy is the worst form of government, except for all those other forms that have been tried from time to time." As usual, Churchill made his audience think about what he had said. Most of his fellow Members of Parliament—and most political observers in the following decades—would probably agree with his view of democracy.

A Clear View

Three centuries earlier, another British leader, Oliver Cromwell, added a new phrase to the English language. Cromwell criticized artist Peter Lily who was painting his portrait. Seeing that the painting made him look more handsome than he really was, Cromwell asked to be depicted realistically, with his irregular face, pimples, and warts. The phrase "warts and all" came from this exchange. It means that people need to see the reality, so they can make up their own minds.

Churchill believed that democracy really was the best form of government, even when judged with warts and all. The "warts" of a democratic system are plain to see. Democracy is a system that reflects public opinion, and this can be harsh, inconsistent, and changeable. Countries sometimes lurch from one type of policy to another, after electing individuals or **parties** with different views from those who previously held power.

The Views of the People

From its roots in ancient Greece to the conflicts of the twenty-first century, democracy is a goal for anyone who wants a government that reflects the views of the people it represents. Abraham Lincoln, who was president of the United States during the **Civil War**, described democracy as "government of the people, by the people, and for the people."

Ultimately, democracy is about choice—being able to choose who leads a country and being able to get rid of leaders when things go wrong. People in democracies exercise their choice by voting. Over the years, the struggle to achieve the vote (for the poor, for women, and other groups) has gone hand in hand with the struggle to introduce democracy.

Modern Democracy

Sometimes democratic elections produce governments that disagree so much that they fall apart within months. For example, Italy had a new government almost every year for much of the second half of the twentieth century. Democratic elections can be influenced by rich people, according to some critics. A successful candidate has to spend hundreds of millions of dollars to become president of the United States. Critics argue that only the rich—or friends of the rich—can raise that sort of money.

This book examines the many criticisms of democracy, while also unveiling the advantages that such an open, and at times, chaotic system gives its citizens. This book seeks to answer why many people without a democratic government strive to achieve it whithin their own countries. What is, then, the secret of this mocked, yet cherished, system of government?

Voters wait patiently outside a Mumbai polling station during state elections in October 2009. India has a population of more than 1.1 billion, and is often described as the world's largest democracy.

Struggling for a Voice

A man carrying only two shopping bags stands in front of an advancing row of tanks in the middle of Tiananmen Square in the Chinese capital, Beijing. The tanks have been called in to crush a protest, but the man stands his ground and the tanks stop. He climbs up on to the first tank, waits for the hatch to be opened, talks with the soldiers inside, and is then escorted away from the area by some concerned bystanders.

The daughter of a much-loved Burmese leader is swept to a decisive election victory, but is then arrested by the Burmese armed forces, and put under house arrest. She goes on to spend 14 of the following years as a prisoner in her own home.

A young black South African defies his country's **racist** laws to become a lawyer. He builds a law practice around helping the poor and needy, often clashing with the whites-only government. He goes on to become a leader of a secret organization devoted to bringing the vote to all South Africans, first going on the run from the police, and then being arrested and serving 27 years in prison. Finally, in his seventies and an international hero, he is victorious in South Africa's first free elections.

Common Themes

These are some of the most recent well-known stories from the long struggle for democracy. The first described one of the most memorable incidents in a series of Chinese pro-democracy protests in 1989. China's communist government responded violently to those protests, although recently, the Chinese people have begun to gain more freedoms.

The second and third stories are about people who have inspired others around the world as they worked to build democracies in their homelands. Aung San Suu Kyi was only two years old when her father, Aung San, who helped guide Burma to independence, was assassinated. Military forces have ruled Burma for nearly 40 years and Aung San's daughter has been a symbol of Burma's

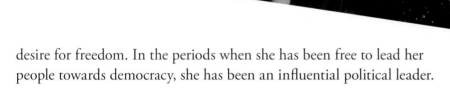

desire for freedom. In the periods when she has been free to lead her people towards democracy, she has been an influential political leader.

Nelson Mandela is one of the most famous people in the world. His commitment to set aside ill feelings in order to work alongside the white South African government has shown him to be an example for others. As president, Mandela was not able to solve all his country's problems, but he opened the door so that South Africans could began to solve them together.

Both Aung San Suu Kyi and Nelson Mandela have been awarded the Nobel Peace Prize, the world's greatest honor for people defending freedom. Although they were born decades apart and a quarter of the globe away from each other, these two people highlight a struggle that has gone on for more than two thousand years—the struggle to let people choose how they will govern themselves.

Aung San Suu Kyi (center) joins senior members of the National League for Democracy to celebrate Burma's Independence Day on January 4, 2011. As leader of the, she has suffered under the military government that rules her country.

MILESTONES LEADING TO THE UNIVERSAL RIGHT TO VOTE

460 BC	Greece: Athens adopts a system of *demokratia* (rule by the people), but it is only for adult male citizens.
287 BC	Rome: Tribunes (officials elected by the people) can make laws in the Roman Republic.
AD 930	Iceland: Althing, the world's oldest parliamentary assembly, is formed.
1832	Britain: The Great Reform Act gives British men who own land the right to vote.
1870	US: Former slaves are given the same voting rights as other US citizens.
1884	Britain: The right to vote is extended to all British adult males.
1890	US: The southern states adopt a poll tax as a way of denying African-Americans the right to vote.
1893	New Zealand: Women earn the right to vote.
1906	Finland: Becomes the first country to give equal voting rights, regardless of wealth or sex.
1918	Britain: Women over the age of 30 win the right to vote.
1920	US: Men and women are given equal voting rights.
1928	Britain: Men and women are given equal voting rights.
1948	The United Nations Universal Declaration of Human Rights calls for "universal and equal **suffrage** in periodic and genuine elections."
1966	US: States can no longer use poll taxes to limit voting rights.
1971	Switzerland: Women gain the same voting rights as men.
1994	South Africa: All people, regardless of race, were allowed to vote for the first time since 1948.

People Power

The word democracy derives from the Greek words *demos* and *kratos*, meaning "people power." The most famous example of ancient democracy developed in the **city-state** of Athens about 2,500 years ago. However, the ancient Athenians had rules about which people deserved this power.

The right to vote in Athens was limited to adult male citizens who were free (not slaves). This meant that only about 12 percent of the population could vote. Based on this evidence, Athenian democracy was not representative of Athens as a whole. On the other hand, the system did ensure that the rich and powerful could not buy votes—an accusation that modern politicians face. Eligible citizens chose lots to decide who would serve on juries and other important decision-making bodies.

Residents of Sandwich, New Hampshire take part in their annual town meeting. Many decisions are voted on democratically at such meetings across the six New England states.

Referendum
on the European Community
(Common Market)

why you
should vote

YES

This is a statement by
Britain in Europe
NOT by HM Government

BRITAIN'S
NEW DEAL
IN EUROPE

'Her Majesty's Government
have decided to recommend
to the British people to vote
for staying in the
Community'

HAROLD WILSON, PRIME M

Referendum
on the European Commun
(Common Market)

why you
should vote

NO

This is a statement by
the National Referendum Campaign
NOT by HM Government

*In 1975, the British government published leaflets to help voters understand why it was holding a **referendum**. Its purpose was to discover what people thought about Britain's role in Europe.*

Later systems of democracy have struggled to find ways to combine being fair and representative with being able to work effectively. The choice is between two forms of democracy, direct and indirect. Parish councils, state and provincial governments, clubs, international organizations, and countries all aim to operate in ways that reflect public opinion while still functioning smoothly.

The Direct Route

Think of all the times people resolve a disagreement by saying, "Let's vote on it." The intended end result is that the group abides by the result of the vote. The process is quick and decisive: identify the alternatives, choose between them, and follow the most popular course.

They might not realize it, but these people's decision making is an example of **direct democracy**—every member of a group has a vote. This is the purest form of democracy. If people agree that it is the purest—and in many ways, fairest—democratic method, then why don't political units and even countries use it?

Some try to do just that, but usually have to settle for less. In some parts of the United States, direct democracy is alive and well in the form of town meetings. Voters in these towns gather regularly to vote on matters that affect them all—whether to raise or lower local taxes, whether to repair the fire station or the school, whether to build a playground or a parking lot. Majority rules in these meetings, and the towns act on the wishes of those who attend the meetings.

Indirect Democracy

The argument against direct democracy is that it becomes unworkable when too many people are involved. Imagine having to vote on every issue—on education, transportation, defense and health policies, for example. No one would have time to do anything, but vote. That is why most countries operate a system of **indirect democracy,** in which voters choose representatives (such as congressional Representatives and Senators or Members of Parliament). They are elected to represent the views of those who chose them, so that those voters' views are taken into account, but indirectly.

Even within these systems, governments can introduce direct democracy. A government might want a major issue to be decided by a vote called a referendum. The United States does not hold referendums at the **federal** level, but many states use referendums to allow citizens to vote on important policies. Recently, issues such as gay marriage, legalizing drugs, and environmental policies have made headlines as certain states have placed them on ballots.

Voting Laws?

Low turnout is a problem for elections in many countries. In some US presidential elections, fewer than half of eligible Americans turn up to vote. As few as 60 percent of British voters bother to vote in some general elections, and the figure is much lower in local and European elections. One solution is to make it illegal not to vote. Australia has such a system, and it is also illegal not to register to vote. Those who fail to do either must pay fines.

Do you think that such a system is the best way to ensure that people's voices are heard? What are the reasons for adopting this approach, what may be some negative effects?

Parliamentary Democracy

Britain has one of the longest unbroken traditions of democracy in the world. The UK government is called a **constitutional monarchy**, which suggests that the king or queen has a part to play in governing the country. In reality, the British monarchy has not played a role in governing for centuries. The ruling British monarch is the head of state, but the governing is done by elected Members of Parliament (MPs). This system is known as parliamentary democracy.

This type of government is centered on the national Parliament. It also involves political parties, as one of the party leaders becomes the country's leader (**prime minister**) after each general election. India, Australia, the Republic of Ireland, and Canada also use this system.

Majority Rules

Usually, the prime minister is the leader of the party that can "command a majority" in Parliament—meaning that its Members of Parliament take up more than half the seats in Parliament. For example, if the prime minister has a majority of 50, and if every MP voted according to the wishes of the party, then the governing party would win each vote in Parliament by at least 50 votes.

MPs do not follow party advice on every vote, but having a big majority means that a party can win votes even if some MPs rebel and vote with opposition parties. Life can be tricky for parties with very small majorities. The government may begin to lose parliamentary votes. Then, the opposition might call a vote of no confidence. If the governing party loses a vote of no confidence, a general election is held.

The UK general election of 2010 produced an unusual result. No party won an outright majority, which meant that two of the parties had to join forces to form a government. This is called a **coalition** (see page 22).

Mamata Banerjee (center), India's Railways Minister, joins colleagues in the midst of India's budget debate. Banerjee is a leading figure in the Trinamed Congress (TMC) party, which has won many parliamentary seats in northeast India.

HOUSE WORK

For centuries, Parliament has been made up of two voting chambers called houses, the House of Lords (or the Upper House) and the House of Commons (or Lower House). Lords and ladies are not elected to their position; they may inherit a title, be appointed to it by the government, or automatically receive a seat in the Upper House because of their position in the Church of England.

The House of Commons reflects popular wishes. Each of the 650 members is elected. In modern Britain, the prime minister is always a member of the Commons, and legislation begins in the Commons. The Upper House has little power to hinder this process, although it can suggest changes to **legislation**.

HER MAJESTY'S OPPOSITION

Under a parliamentary system, general elections can be called suddenly, even before a parliament is due to end its **term**. A vote of no confidence can force an election, or a prime minister can call a snap election if the time seems right to make the best of some favorable news. In either case, the election takes place within weeks.

Sudden elections can lead to chaos if the governing party is voted out and the victorious party has to start from scratch in choosing people to make up the **cabinet**. That is why the government's main rival party chooses its own people to take on important jobs, such as **foreign secretary** or **chancellor of the exchequer**. These people are called shadow foreign secretary, and so on, and they stand by to take over cabinet positions if their party should win the next election. This shadow cabinet forms part of the **official opposition**, officially known as Her Majesty's opposition in the British system.

The role of the opposition is to ask questions about a government's proposed legislation, contributing opinions and advice so that every aspect of an issue is explored. In reality, the opposition often waits to take advantage of mistakes made by the government, hoping to influence public opinion in their favor.

The executioner holds up the head of King Charles I, who was beheaded on the orders of the English Parliament in 1649. There had been years of civil war between forces loyal to the king and those of Parliament, and power was now in the hands of the people.

MILESTONES IN PARLIAMENTARY DEMOCRACY

1265 First English Parliament with elected members meets.

1326 First Scottish Parliament meets.

1362 English (rather than Norman French) becomes the official language of English Parliament.

1605 Members of the Gunpowder Plot (which aimed to blow up Parliament) are caught and executed.

1629 King Charles I of England **dissolves** Parliament in a show of strength.

1640 King Charles I is forced to recall Parliament to raise funds to fight a Scottish rebellion.

1641 Civil war between supporters of the king and those of Parliament spreads from England to other parts of Britain and Ireland.

1649 Parliamentary forces convict Charles I of treason and execute him.

1689 A Bill of Rights limits the power of the monarchy over Parliament.

1707 English and Scottish Parliaments are united.

1721 Robert Walpole becomes the first British prime minister.

1803 William Cobbett begins unofficial publication of parliamentary reports.

1978 Regular broadcasting of proceedings in Parliament begins.

1979 First direct elections for the European Parliament held.

1998 National Assembly for Wales is established.

1999 Official opening of new Scottish Parliament.

2010 Conservatives and Liberal Democrats form a coalition government.

Hail to the Chief

Many people describe British parliamentary democracy as a happy accident. It works largely because it reflects centuries of trial and error. Along the way, it picked up traditions that seem to have little to do with democracy, such as the involvement of the monarchy and unelected officials being able to influence law-making. The British **constitution** is unwritten, meaning that political experts have to look for similar examples in past centuries to resolve problems.

Spelling Things Out

Americans lived under the British parliamentary system until the late 1700s, when the United States became independent. The new government decided to use some elements of the British system, mixed with political ideas of their own. The present system of American government goes back to the **founding fathers**, who spelled things out in a written constitution.

The United States has no king, still the elected president has many of the same state responsibilities as the British monarch. However, unlike the British monarch, the US president is directly involved in the business of government. He or she stands at the head of the **executive branch**, one of the three main branches of government. The other two branches are the **legislative branch** (the two houses of Congress), and the **judicial branch** (judges and courts). The president also acts as the Commander in Chief of the US Armed Forces, and is involved with military decisions.

Checks and Balances

The US system of government is known as a presidential democracy, but in practice, it is designed to be a partnership between the three main branches of government, so that no single branch becomes too powerful. The president, for example, can vote down, or veto, a law passed by Congress. Or the judicial branch can decide to overturn a law (which might have been approved by both the president and Congress), because it is unconstitutional.

Supporters of Brazil's Workers' Party celebrate the victory of their party leader, Dilma Rousseff, in the October 2010 general election.

VOICE OF THE PEOPLE

LOCAL KNOWLEDGE

Sometimes voters are surprised to see one of their local politicians gaining power on the national stage. When Franklin Pierce, a man of few words, became US president in 1832, one farmer from his home state was quoted as saying: "That feller Pierce was all right here in New Hampshire, but I reckon that when he gets to Washington, he's going to be spread durned thin."

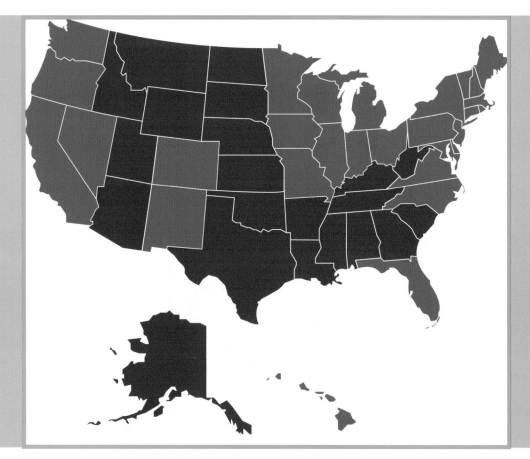

Each of the 50 states in the United States has been colored to show the result of the 2008 presidential election. States that voted for the Democratic candidate (Barack Obama) have been colored blue. Those that chose the Republican candidate (John McCain) are colored red.

With each branch keeping tabs on the others, a system called checks and balances is created. Each branch can check the power of the others in order to maintain the overall balance. This system is a response to the British system. Many Americans believe that a parliamentary democracy lacks such balance because the prime minister can usually be assured of getting legislation passed by Parliament.

Grinding to a Halt?

On the other hand, people living in parliamentary democracies can observe how the American system becomes bogged down at times. President Barack Obama, who was elected in 2008, had promised sweeping changes to the American health system during his campaign. In the same election, Obama's Democratic party had gained majorities in both the US Senate and House of Representatives.

A swift change in the American system seemed promising, but every single Republican decided to vote against the health bill. Then, a number of Democrats also said they would vote against it. Obama's proposal was soon in danger of being strangled at birth. It was only after a series of compromises that the bill was passed in early 2010.

Another Democratic president, Bill Clinton, had also faced a tough battle also with health care 16 years earlier. Two years after Clinton was elected president in 1992, the Republicans gained control of both houses in congressional elections. Clinton's health proposal was voted down along with many of his other proposals.

THE ELECTORAL COLLEGE

The United States has always tried to find political balance between the power of individual states and of the national government. When presidential elections are held every four years, Americans vote state by state rather than nationally to choose their president. The presidential candidate who wins the most votes in a particular state receives all the electoral votes for that state—ranging from a handful to a few dozen, depending on the population.

Whoever wins most of these votes, which are recorded in what is known as the **electoral college**—becomes president. It is possible to be elected president without having the highest **popular vote**, as George W. Bush did in 2000. That election showed how an entire presidential election can be decided by just a few votes in a single state (see pages 32–33).

THE VOTING BOOTH

King George I?

After George Washington led America's army to independence from Great Britain, he became a national hero. Most Americans wanted him to lead their new country, and some people believed that he should become king. Washington refused to consider such a position; instead he was elected as the first president of the United States. How might the United States have developed if Washington had become king rather than president? Would the role of kings gradually have become symbolic, as it has in constitutional monarchies such as Britain's? Or do you think Americans might prefer a strong monarch?

Mixing and Matching

Democracy is about choice. Like any group of people trying to come to an agreement, voters might not come to a firm decision. Uncertainty and disagreement are not good ingredients for effective government, so political leaders need to find ways of translating the voters' wishes into a practical way of operating. One solution is to "go to the people" whenever confusion develops, which might mean holding another election soon after an inconclusive one—sometimes only months later. Another solution is for different parties, which normally oppose each other, to work together as a coalition.

Above: Protesters in Brussels, wearing Belgian national colors, call for national unity rather than party rivalry after the ruling coalition fell apart in April 2010.

Left: Young British voters engage in a mock swordfight on the lawn outside the Houses of Parliament two days before the 2010 general election. Kidding aside, the protest had a serious underlying message supporting the prospect of a hung parliament.

The Way Ahead or Stalemate?

In the British general election of 1997, the Labour Party was swept to power. It was very popular at first, as it seemed to bring a sense of youth and change to the country. Pop stars and actors mingled with members of the new Labour government at social events in 1997, and many British people were genuinely excited about the future.

By 2010, however, the national mood had changed. Many Labour supporters felt the government had not met their expectations. The world was in the middle of an economic crisis, and many British people thought the government had made the situation worse by borrowing far too much money. The Labour Party was showing signs of disagreement; some senior Labour politicians were calling for the prime minister, Gordon Brown, to step down as leader. Meanwhile, the other main British political parties—the Conservatives and the Liberal Democrats—had persuasive, young leaders.

The stage was set for a demonstration of how the British parliamentary democracy could adjust to voters' fast-moving attitudes. British voters were to choose a new government on May 6, 2010. In previous elections, a government led by an unpopular party had been replaced by the main opposition party. That pattern was likely to make David Cameron, the leader of the Conservatives, prime minister on May 7.

But on May 7, things looked far less clear. The Conservatives had indeed done better than the Labour party. They had won 306 seats compared with 258 won by the Labour party. But that was still 20 short of "one more than half," the definition of a parliamentary majority. With no party able to form a government immediately, the result was a **hung parliament**.

Unexpected Pairings

The Liberal Democrats had received 23 percent of the vote, which only translated to 57 seats. However, those seats could secure a strong position for one of the other parties. The Conservative and Labour parties then considered working with the Liberal Democrats to form a coalition government, something that the UK had not seen since the 1940s.

Nick Clegg, the Liberal Democrat leader, had said he would discuss a coalition with the party that received the most votes. That led to the Conservative-Liberal Democrat Coalition Agreement, announced six days after the election. Both parties proved willing to compromise by accepting policies that they had opposed throughout the run up to the election.

It seems unimaginable to many US and British voters that former opponents can team up to govern, but it is a common occurrence in many countries. Countries usually run by coalition governments tend to have voting systems that allow smaller parties to win seats. Unlike the "first past the post" system that is common in the United States and the United Kingdom, these systems offer variations of **proportional representation**, sometimes simply called PR.

Critics of PR say that it leads to permanent crisis, with governments hanging by a thread and the threat of new elections always just around the corner. They point to Italy and Israel where small political parties—sometimes with extreme views—can hold the balance of power. Supporters counter by saying that Germany, the Netherlands, and the Republic of Ireland, with PR produce stable governments. Another advantage is that the parties realize they must always be willing to compromise and to respect each other.

Israeli prime minister Yitzhak Rabin (right) and foreign minister Shimon Peres attend a meeting of the Knesset (parliament) in October 1995. Israeli politics is dominated by coalitions and fierce rivalries. Rabin was assassinated by a political extremist several weeks later.

THE VOTING BOOTH

Measuring Democracy?

The *Economist* magazine regularly produces a Democracy Index, which aims to be a scientific study of the world's governments. It rates each system on how democratic it is according to many categories such as free elections, active newspapers, open government, and so on. How accurate do you think measures such as the Democracy Index really are? Do you believe that a country's political leaders worry about how democratic their systems are? Might voters use such an index to press for more freedom and openness? Is it impossible to measure something like democracy?

International Cooperation

In many ways, countries behave like individual people. They buy and sell goods and services, agree or disagree with each other, but generally try to live among others peacefully. Over the last 60 years, the world's many countries have formed organizations to build economic ties and to promote peace. In the twentieth century, millions of people died due to conflicts, including two world wars. Today's international organizations were formed to prevent similar bloodshed.

No one would argue against either prosperity or peace, yet the organizations that have been set up to achieve those goals have

Good for Democracy?

Many Americans resent criticism of their country's foreign policy from some members of the United Nations. Likewise, **Eurosceptics** in Britain complain about the increasing role of the **European Union** and the way in which it influences British life. Do you think that strong international organizations help to build democracy on a global scale, or do they trample democratic traditions on a national scale?

Palestinian president Mahmoud Abbas addresses the United Nations General Assembly in October 2009. The General Assembly is the parliament of the UN, and each of the 192 members—rich or poor, large or small—has one vote.

been criticized very strongly. Some Americans believe the most famous organization, the United Nations (UN), is anti-American, and that its decisions reflect this stance. They argue that many decisions made by their democratically elected US government have been voted against by representatives of undemocratic countries who belong to the UN.

Opponents of that view say that the UN, like other international organizations, offers countries a chance to behave in a democratic fashion among themselves, so the majority rules. They argue that without organizations such as the UN, large and powerful countries would always have their own way. In particular, supporters of international organizations see parallels with the democratic system of the United States (see page 27). They compare the position of small countries such as Iceland, Tunisia, and Bolivia with that of states such as Idaho, Vermont, and Iowa. Those smaller states (or countries) cannot expect to control their larger counterparts, but by grouping together democratically, they can build their influence.

European Politics

Similar arguments are common in any discussion of European politics. Many Europeans take the view that unelected officials from the European Union (EU) run their lives. The Belgian capital, Brussels, is where many EU decisions are made. Many British Eurosceptics believe that those decisions often overrule those of the British Parliament. Much of the British media reflects this anti-EU viewpoint, publishing stories about "new rulings from Brussels" that outlaw pint glasses, open Britain's doors to more **immigrants,** and even dictate the shape of bananas that can be sold.

Eurosceptics—opponents of close British links with the EU—use patriotic symbols and themes to promote their views. This man is dressed in the costume of John Bull, a traditional symbol of British resolve, to stage a protest against the European common currency, the Euro.

Even if some of those objections seem silly or exaggerated, they reflect an underlying fear. Some EU supporters would welcome a "United States of Europe" built along the lines of the American federal system, but Eurosceptics would view this as a nightmare.

The global economic difficulties since 2007 have heightened some of the tensions between those who support closer European ties and those who oppose them. Several countries along the outer edge of the EU—especially Greece, Ireland, and Portugal have experienced severe economic problems.

Those economic difficulties have been so problematic that they have threatened to endanger the entire Eurozone (the collection of countries that adopted the Euro as a common European currency). The EU has been forced to come up with rescue plans to protect itself. These plans often involve big loans to troubled governments.

Opponents of European integration, and especially British opponents of the Euro, have seen this crisis as evidence that the European ideal is failing. They have strengthened their anti-Euro protests as a result.

FEDERAL SYSTEMS

People who live in a remote region of a country can easily believe that they are denied a voice by a government based in a faraway capital. Their region has few voters compared with more populated industrial regions, and such regions often accuse the central government of ignoring their needs and wishes. If the United States had only a central government, then people in places such as Wyoming and Alaska would have less influence than their counterparts in heavily populated California and New York.

The American system of democracy faced this problem from the moment the country became independent more than 200 years ago. The 13 colonies that became the first 13 states would never have agreed to group together as a country unless some sort of balance had been achieved between the big and the small. One solution lies in the state-by-state system of electing the US president, called the electoral college (see page 19). Another lies in the make-up of the federal system.

The two houses of the US Congress show the mixture at work. The number of representatives each state elects to Congress depends on that state's population. California, New York, and Texas have far more representatives than Wyoming, Vermont, or Utah. But each state elects two US senators, so the smaller states have an equal say in America's upper house. States also have their own state governments, which can raise taxes, build roads and schools, and make laws about important issues such as the death penalty. Meanwhile, the federal (or national) government decides on national matters such as the economy and foreign policy.

The United States is probably the most famous example of a federal system of government, but there are other countries which divide power between central and regional governments in federal systems. Many countries with federal systems, such as Germany, India, Australia, and Canada, operate parliamentary-style democracies.

Does Democracy Work?

Many historians believe that the word demokratia (people power) might have originally been a term of abuse. For a society accustomed to strong, unelected leaders (which was true of many Greek city-states, including Athens), waiting to vote on every important decision could seem inefficient. More worrying was the idea of allowing inexperienced people to have a say in all sorts of areas: choosing trading partners, deciding on religious observation, and going to war.

The alternative to letting ignorant people have a say in government would be to adopt a system of enlightened despotism, in which a well-informed (or well-advised) ruler would have the final say in such decisions. This course of action is tempting, especially if a democratically elected government seems to be indecisive or ineffective. Perhaps firm leadership is the only way forward, some people conclude.

Boys play with kites made from worthless banknotes in 1920s Germany. Such extreme economic failure paved the way for Hitler to be elected leader.

James Michael Curley was elected Mayor of Boston, Massachusetts, four times despite having been sent to prison twice during his political career.

Germany in the 1920s was an example of an ineffective society. The German economy was still crippled by the aftermath of World War I. High unemployment and **inflation** made many people feel helpless and depressed. It was in those circumstances that Adolf Hitler came to power. His Nazi party gained power in national elections in the early 1930s, but soon abandoned democratic principles as Hitler gained more and more power. By the end of that decade, Hitler had triggered another world war, which would prove to be a threat to democracy across Europe and beyond.

Mob Rule

Democracies face other accusations. At its most basic level, democracy faces the charge of promoting "mob rule." A mob, of course, is a wild and brutal crowd with little respect for individuals or anything else. By allowing the majority to influence decisions, critics say, a democracy can be dominated by brutal and powerful elements within it.

An Italian soldier, a member of an international peace-keeping force, patrols a village in Afghanistan in 2010. The peace-keepers are trying to help Afghanistan restore democratic rule after years of civil war and terrorism.

In the early decades of the twentieth century, many American cities were run by "political machines," the term used to describe unofficial (and often illegal) political groups that supported certain candidates. On the surface, these machines operated within legal democratic limits, providing advertising for their favored candidates, driving elderly people to voting stations, and so forth. Very often, though, they used unfair or illegal tactics to gain an advantage, such as bullying opponents, lying about their candidate's achievements, and even destroying ballots with votes for their opponents. In some cities, people registered to vote under several names, which led to the saying, "vote early and vote often."

Nowadays, such tactics are less likely to be used in the United States and in other countries with stable democratic governments. However, some countries are only now entering a democratic era after years of colonialism, warfare, or dictatorships. Afghanistan and Iraq are two examples of fragile democracies, threatened every day by terrorism, internal divisions, corruption, and tribal rivalries. Many other countries are also trying to nurture democracies in the face of menacing obstacles.

VOICE OF THE PEOPLE

A STRUGGLE BETRAYED

Marcus Jameson (his name has been changed to protect his safety) is a white Zimbabwean who grew up at a time when his country was called Rhodesia and was ruled by a whites-only government. He welcomed the transition from Rhodesia to Zimbabwe in the early 1980s, but he is saddened by the way the country has since fallen victim to corruption and violence.

"Our family always felt that our black neighbors were denied a chance to build a future for themselves because of the racist government of Rhodesia. When Robert Mugabe (the former rebel leader who became president soon after independence) came to power, we welcomed him as much as black Zimbabweans. Sure, we felt a little squeezed as it became harder to get some of the jobs that had once been reserved for whites. But that old system was wrong, and we felt that we were building a new democracy alongside our black neighbors.

"So it was a particularly bitter pill to swallow as we watched a lot of those hopes go down the drain in the decades since then. Many whites have fled out of fear. We've stayed because we still want to play a part in our country, but it's sad to see the struggle to build democracy dishonored so brutally."

Free Choice?

The United Nations and other international organizations often send observers to make sure elections in newly independent countries are conducted properly. At face value, this seems an admirable way of spreading and preserving democracy. However, critics argue that some nations want no part of democracy, because they prefer to be governed along religious or tribal lines. If these countries had wanted democracies, the critics argue, they would have chosen to form democratic governments on their own years ago. Critics believe any outside involvement amounts to interference. What do you think?

Does My Vote Really Count?

Winston Churchill wove an important truth into that clever saying when he described democracy. No system is perfect, and sometimes democracy loses sight of its ideal of representing the people's will. Election results sometimes go directly against the people's choice.

Close Calls

In 2000, George W. Bush was elected president of the United States with only 5 more electoral votes than his opponent Al Gore. Bush won the electoral college, despite Gore winning more than half of one million more popular votes than Bush. While 500,000 votes

sounds like quite a lot, the result came to Bush taking 47.87 percent of the votes, and Gore winning 48.38 percent of the vote. The results were very close, and each candidate questioned if there was a possibility for a miscount.

One state that had a particularly close race was Florida, where only a few hundred votes separated the candidates. Florida's 25 electoral votes would decide who won the election. A **recount** was called to verify the results. After weeks of counting and analyzing ballots, Bush was named the winner of the popular vote in Florida by 537 votes, and therefore winner of the 25 electoral votes. Those 537 voters in Florida certainly made a difference in that election.

Third Parties

A problem with some elections is that, while majority rules, the winner doesn't always get the majority of the vote. The 2008 Senate race in Minnesota resulted in Democrat Al Franken and Republican

The 2000 US presidential election hinged on whether George W. Bush or Al Gore had won more votes in Florida. Officials had to check whether ballots had been punched through completely (which would count as a vote) or were simply pressed hard (which would not). The state decided that out of nearly 6 million votes that had been cast, Bush received 537 more than Gore.

THE LOBBY SYSTEM

One of the charges against a democratic government is that it allows rich individuals or companies to use their wealth to influence voters or their representatives. Many corporations employ people known as **lobbyists** to present their case to representatives. This term comes from the public lobby in the British Parliament, where members of the public can approach members of parliament.

Over the course of a dinner, a round of golf, or some other form of entertainment, lobbyists spell out how a bill being discussed is either a good or bad thing, and why they think the representative should vote in a certain way. Most of the time, lobbyists do nothing illegal in trying to influence opinions in this way, but many observers believe that lobbying is still a way of buying influence.

Britain's first televised leaders' debate during a general election took place on April 15, 2010. Nick Clegg, leader of the Liberal Democrats (left), David Cameron of the Conservatives (center), and Gordon Brown of the Labour Party (right) all took part.

Norm Coleman each taking about 42 percent of the votes. Independent candidate Dean Barkley won about 15 percent of the votes. Al Franken was declared the winner of the Senate seat, even though 58 percent of Minnesotans did not vote for him.

While voters should cast ballots for the person they truly want to lead, many voters will avoid voting for a candidate that is unlikely to win. They feel their vote is wasted on an underdog third-party candidate, and therefore, essentially, feel voting for third parties only causes a winner who most people did not vote for.

VOTER RIGHTS IN THE UNITED STATES

In an ideal democracy, every citizen would have a voice. This has not been the case in any democratic system, and sadly in some situations, the very government that is supposed to represent the people has created laws and practices that purposely limit the ability for some citizens to vote. Before the US Civil War (1861–1865), there were no federal laws about voter rights. Each state made their own rules, and often, states only allowed free men who owned property to register and vote in elections. However, the 15th Amendment was ratified in 1870, and stated that the right to vote could not be denied based on race, color, or whether the person was previously a slave.

Many southern states had very large black populations, and discrimination was very prevalent. People did not want blacks to vote for officials who would work to give equality to them. States came up with all sorts of requirements for voter registration. Some requirements included passing a literacy test and paying a poll tax. People who could not read well enough, did not complete a certain amount of schooling, or could not afford to pay the tax were deemed ineligible to vote. While these rules appear to be valid ways of ensuring that only informed citizens are voting, they were specifically designed to find ways to make black Americans ineligible to vote.

By 1920, American women had won the right to vote, but it wasn't until 1964 that the 24th Amendment was ratified, outlawing poll taxes as a requirement for federal voting rights. The Voting Rights Act was passed in 1965 further outlawing discriminating practices for voter registration. In 1966, the Supreme Court ruled that any poll taxes and other discriminatory registration requirements at the state and local levels were also illegal.

While discrimination is still a problem in the United States, the Voting Rights Act and the Supreme Court decisions regarding voting rights have been some of the most effective ways of ensuring equal civil rights for all Americans.

Democracy
and the Media

Democracy is about choice. Unlike people living in countries where power is controlled by individuals or small groups, citizens governed by democratic systems expect to choose their leaders by voting them into office. They should also be able to "throw the rascals out"—as the saying goes—by voting them out of office.

Anyone making a choice needs to know what the alternatives are. People deciding which movie to see will base their judgement on reviews they read, advertisements, or the recommendations of their friends. Voters deciding who to vote for in a democratic election

SEEING IS BELIEVING

The US presidential election of 1960 was one of the closest in history. The Democratic party candidate, John F. Kennedy, defeated the Republican, Richard M. Nixon, by only one percentage point. Midway through their campaign, Kennedy's aides proposed something new and untested—a televised debate.

Nixon, who was already vice-president and had proved himself a skilled debater, agreed, but he and his team made a number of mistakes, which worked to Kennedy's advantage. Nixon was made up to highlight the fact that he was older than Kennedy (who, Nixon believed, would look inexperienced). Instead, the makeup made him look stern and angry under the harsh television lights. Nixon also emphasized the seriousness of the issues by pointing his finger at Kennedy and scowling at times. Kennedy, on the other hand, looked directly at the cameras so that he seemed to be talking directly to the American people, as a friend might.

The Americans who listened to the Nixon-Kennedy debate on the radio considered Nixon to be the winner. However, the novelty of a televised debate meant that 70 million people—two-thirds of America's voters—watched it on television. In polls taken after the debate, they judged Kennedy to be the victor. Ever since, no major candidate in any democracy has been able to ignore the power of television.

John F. Kennedy (left) was far more comfortable in a series of television debates than his opponent Richard Nixon. Kennedy's confidence and youthful appearance swayed many voters, helping him to be elected US president in 1960.

WISE WORDS

"There are only two forces that can carry light to all corners of the globe, and only two: the sun in the heavens and the Associated Press down here."

American writer Mark Twain, in a speech in 1906.

also need information about the candidates before making their final choice. They depend on television, radio, newspapers, magazines, and the Internet to learn about candidates and the issues that define and divide them.

Two-Way Street

For people in democratic countries, this flow of information is normal and forms part of their lives. A free press is one of the most basic rights in a democracy. It is vital for reporters to be able to uncover the truth behind important stories. Newspapers carry stories on the reasons a nation has gone to war, how a particular builder won the contract to build a new hospital, or how much taxpayer money has been used to settle a long-running dispute about workers' injuries.

As a result, many politicians have come to view the media with suspicion. They might expect to be accused of greed or stupidity when they meet a reporter. It is hardly surprising, then, that undemocratic governments ban opposition newspapers and television networks. The media in these countries come under direct government control, and so the people mistrust the information they are given. Even within democratic countries, some politicians have been able to use the media to give them an advantage.

Singers Taboo (left) and Andy Vargas (right) join guitarist and composer George Pajon, Jr. (center) to record a Spanish-language version of Barack Obama's campaign song "Yes We Can" (Si Se Puede) during the 2008 presidential election. The song aimed to persuade Spanish-speaking voters to vote for Obama.

THE VOTING BOOTH

The First Casualty

People say that the truth is the first **casualty** in times of war. Governments and military leaders often impose limits on what journalists report about the fighting. The intention is to keep public confidence high. Many argue that restrictions are a form of censorship that denies people their democratic right to information. Such disputes become especially heated when a war is unpopular with many citizens—as has been the case in Iraq and Afghanistan, for example.

Do you believe that there should be some limits, in order to maintain morale and to protect the lives of those in the armed forces? Or should journalists be able to report freely to allow or enabling the public to decide how to conduct a war?

Journalists by a mass grave, thought to contain up to 600 Kuwaiti prisoners of war executed in 1991 in Habbaniya, near Baghdad, in May 2003.

Voters of the Future

Young people have many opportunities to shape their democratic surroundings—opportunities that their parents or grandparents could not have imagined when they were young. Perhaps most importantly, new types of technology have been driving the democratic process forward. Young people are usually on the cutting edge of each new advance, whether it is cell phones, blogging, iPads, or social network websites.

Youth protest the education cuts proposed by the French government in late 2010. The French, like many other governments, have responded to the global economic crisis by cutting spending in many areas.

Much of this activity has helped to inject new life into fully functioning democracies. Supporters of Barack Obama, for example, used the Internet to spread their candidate's message and to raise record amounts for campaign funds. Just as John F. Kennedy and Nick Clegg used the power of television to their advantage (see pages 34–37), the successful candidates of the future will be those who can harness new technology.

Brave young people in harsher regimes are using the new technology in their struggle just to introduce democracy. Many of the pro-democracy uprisings in Tunisia, Egypt, Bahrain, and Libya that captured world interest in 2011 were organized and encouraged through messages via Twitter, Facebook, and other social network websites.

Whether the subject is called citizenship, civics, or government, most democratic countries aim to educate their young people about politics with classes at school. Some young people become inspired to play a more active part in the political process. Established political parties often have youth sections that encourage membership and involvement in campaigns. Other politically minded young people can get a feel for the political process by taking part in organizations, such as the Model United Nations.

THE VOTING BOOTH

Votes at 16

Some young people are not content simply learning about how their government works so they will be well informed by the time they are old enough to vote. They want to be able to vote once they reach the age of 16. Votes at 16 is a British organization with the goal of lowering the voting age from 18 to 16. The argument they put forward asks why, if people can sign up to go to war at 16, they are not considered old enough to vote at that age? What do you think?

Looking Ahead

People can get things spectacularly wrong when they try to predict the future. Some experts in the 1950s, for example, predicted that computers would remain so huge and expensive that only four or five would be used in each country. Others believed that by the year 2000, families would have their own flying cars and humans would have built cities on the moon and Mars.

A Vote for Change in Britain?

The formation of a coalition government in 2010 could have been the first step in a long road towards voting-system change in Great Britain. The Conservative Party needed to offer some **concessions** to the Liberal Democrats to draw them into a coalition. One of the biggest was agreeing to a national referendum on changing the British voting system.

For decades, the Liberal Democrats had been squeezed by Britain's "first past the post" electoral system. The two bigger parties—Labour and Conservative—won the most parliamentary seats because the candidate with the most votes won the seat, even if he or she only won by one vote. But the Liberal Democrats often came a strong second, outscoring the losing candidates by thousands of votes. Although the Liberal Democrats had support across the country—about 20 percent of the overall vote—some people felt that a vote for them was a wasted vote.

On May 5, 2011, British voters were given the chance to choose a form of proportional representation in a national referendum. The result, however, strongly supported the existing system by more than two to one: 32 percent voted for change and 67 percent wanted to retain the existing system. Was that the last word on the debate, or might another system be proposed in the future?

A Gay Pride parade makes its way through a slum on the outskirts of Rio de Janeiro in October 2010. Modern democracies celebrate the richness and variety of their societies, where in the past, minorities, such as homosexuals, might have felt excluded.

Both predictions seem wildly off the mark, and yet they were based on a close study of technology. Think how much more difficult it is to predict people's behavior and opinions, considering how often people change their minds. Therefore, a political system such as democracy, which is linked to public opinion, must be almost impossible to predict.

Or is it? Many people believe history is a process of conflict, and each struggle has eventually led to a victory for democracy. Historian Francis Fukuyama has gone so far as to claim that history as we know it has ended and democracy has finally won the battle (see The Voting Booth, page 45).

International versus National Levels

It seems impossible to predict the overall progress of democracy around the world. We don't know which countries will adopt democracy and which will lose it to more **authoritarian** forms of government. Political

observers can detect trends, and they see ideas from one country transferred to others very quickly. For example, once some European countries began to give women the right to vote in the early twentieth century, others quickly followed.

Another example is a scandal in Britain during 2009 and 2010. People learned that members of parliament from all parties had used official funds to pay private expenses. The coalition government formed after the 2010 general election promised to crack down on such behavior, adopting measures already used in Australia, the United States, and Canada.

Established democracies, such as those in the United States and Great Britain, have survived many scandals, and will continue to thrive. The real tests of democracy are for countries that are relatively new to it. They need to convince their people that openness and free choice are the best ways towards success in the twenty-first century.

VOICE OF THE PEOPLE

DELIVERING RESULTS

Nigeria, which has more people than any other country in Africa, has had a democratic government since 1999, when the previous military government allowed open elections. Since then, however, the democratic government has been accused of corruption and inefficiency. Moses Ochonu, a Nigerian political expert, believes that democracy must deliver results if it is to survive in Nigeria: "Our perception of democracy is a purely utilitarian one. Americans [continually debate] what democracy means; Nigerians ask what it can deliver to them. Nigerians evaluate democratic practice not in abstract or futuristic terms but in terms of its immediate benefits to their lives. Democracy will only be as popular as the results it delivers for Nigerians."

Soldiers from Nigeria guard the office of General Salou Djibo of neighboring Niger, who led the overthrow of Mamadou Tandja in February 2010. Tandja had been planning to remain in power longer than the term he won in the 2004 general election. Djibo led the overthrow, which helped to restore democracy and full democratic elections in Niger in 2011.

THE VOTING BOOTH

The End of History?

In 1992, the American historian Francis Fukuyama claimed the end of history had arrived. For him, history had been a long process of struggle between competing systems of government. The unraveling of the Soviet Union the year before, along with most communist governments, had convinced him that the struggle was over. Communism, the biggest rival to democratic government, had collapsed. Now there was no enemy to threaten democracy, and without the struggle history ceased to exist.

Do you agree with his conclusions? Do you think anything has changed since 1992 that would make Fukuyama change his mind?

Glossary

authoritarian   An authoritarian government uses force to rule.

cabinet   A high-ranking group of officials who discuss national issues and plan government action.

casualty   A victim (killed or wounded) in a war.

chancellor of the exchequer   The cabinet member in charge of the British economy.

citizens   People who have a say in how their country is governed, especially by being able to vote.

city-state   A self-governing region built around a powerful city.

Civil War   A war fought in the United States (1861–65) when 11 states tried to break away from the country.

coalition   A teaming-up of two or more parties to form a government.

concession   Something that is given, usually in response to demands, to persuade someone to agree to something.

constitution   A document outlining how an organization (or country) is to be governed.

constitutional monarchy   A democratic system that has a king or queen, but only in a symbolic role.

direct democracy   A system in which people vote directly on each issue.

dissolve (of a parliament)   To break apart and bring to a close.

electoral college   A body of people who represent the states of the US, who vote for the president and the vice-president. The number of votes each state casts depends on the size of its population.

European Union   A group of 25 European countries that work together on political and economic matters.

Eurosceptics   People who do not want their country to give more power to the European Union.

executive branch   The branch of government relating to the president and his or her advisers.

federal   a central government that oversees the individual regional governments.

foreign secretary   The British cabinet member in charge of deciding on Britain's role in the world.

founding fathers   The American political leaders who founded the US government after winning independence from Britain in the late eighteenth century.

French Revolution   A political upheaval, beginning in 1789, which overthrew the French monarchy and established a democracy.

general election   An election that decides who will form a government to rule a country.

hung parliament   The result of an election that fails to give any single party enough seats to form a government automatically.

immigrants   People who travel from another country to live in this one.

indirect democracy   A political system in which people elect representatives to vote on issues.

inflation   An increase in prices and a fall in the value of money.

judicial branch   The branch of government concerned with judges and courts.

legislation   Law-making as voted on by elected representatives.

legislative branch   The branch of government that produces legislation.

lobbyist   Someone who is paid to try to influence elected representatives.

official opposition   Members of the largest party in Parliament that opposes the current government.

parties   Organizations with shared political views and the goal of getting their members elected to government.

popular vote   The total number of people who vote for a person or party

prime minister   The leader of the majority party in Parliament, who also becomes national leader.

proportional representation   A voting system that tries to match the number of seats won by a party to that party's share of the vote.

racist   Favoring one group of people over others, based on their race.

recount   A second counting of votes after a close election.

referendum   A special vote, usually on a single issue, so that all voters can register a view.

register   Sign up to the official list of voters in an area.

statesman   A high-ranking and respected political leader.

suffrage   The right to vote.

term   The length of time an elected official has in office before another person could be elected.

Books

Downing, David. *Democracy (Political and Econimic Systems)*. Heinemann, 2008.
Rees, Peter. *Liberty: Blessing or Burden (Shockwave)*. Children's Press, 2008.
O'Donnell, Liam. *Democracy (Graphic Library. Cartoon Nation)*. Capstone Press, 2008.

Websites

The Democracy Project
http://pbskids.org/democracy

Votes at 16
http://votesat16.org.uk

Model UN
http://www.unausa.org/modelun

Index